WRITTEN BY EMILY KINGTON
ILLUSTRATED BY DUSAN LAKICEVIC

MY FIRST BOOK OF
BUGS

CONTENTS

Words in BOLD can be found in the glossary.

WHAT ARE BUGS?

Bugs are all AROUND US!

Our planet is crawling with bugs; wherever you go in the world you will find them!

Bugs are the best!

There are millions of different bugs, from creepy-crawly spiders to busy buzzy insects, wiggly worms to slimy slugs. They all have different features and skills that make them special.

Bug hunt

You can find them underground, in the air, in the water, and even in your home!

What makes an insect an insect?

All insects have three body parts: a head, thorax, and abdomen. They can also have wings, six legs, and antennae.

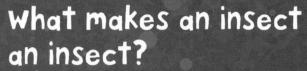

Antenna

Thorax

Head

Leg

Abdomen

Wing

Not all bugs are insects, but lots of them are! Turn the page to discover some super busy bugs.

ANT

Ants are EVERYWHERE!

They live in groups, called colonies, and build nests with lots of tunnels. Some nests have more than one million ants living inside them!

Antennae for feeling and smelling things

DID YOU KNOW?

I eat... almost anything! Including leaves, seeds, small insects, tree **sap**, and fruit.

I have... 6 legs!

I can be found... in nests underground, in trees, or even inside some plants.

I grow up to... 2 inches (4cm).

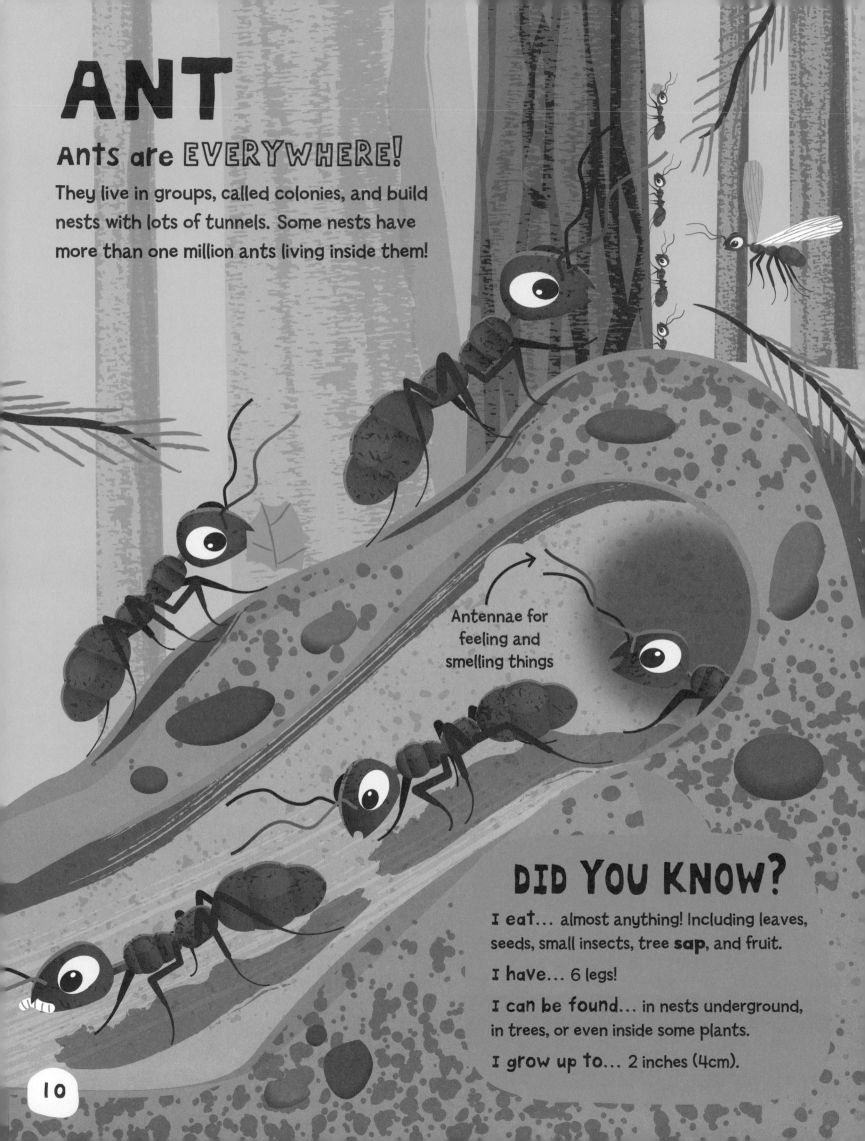

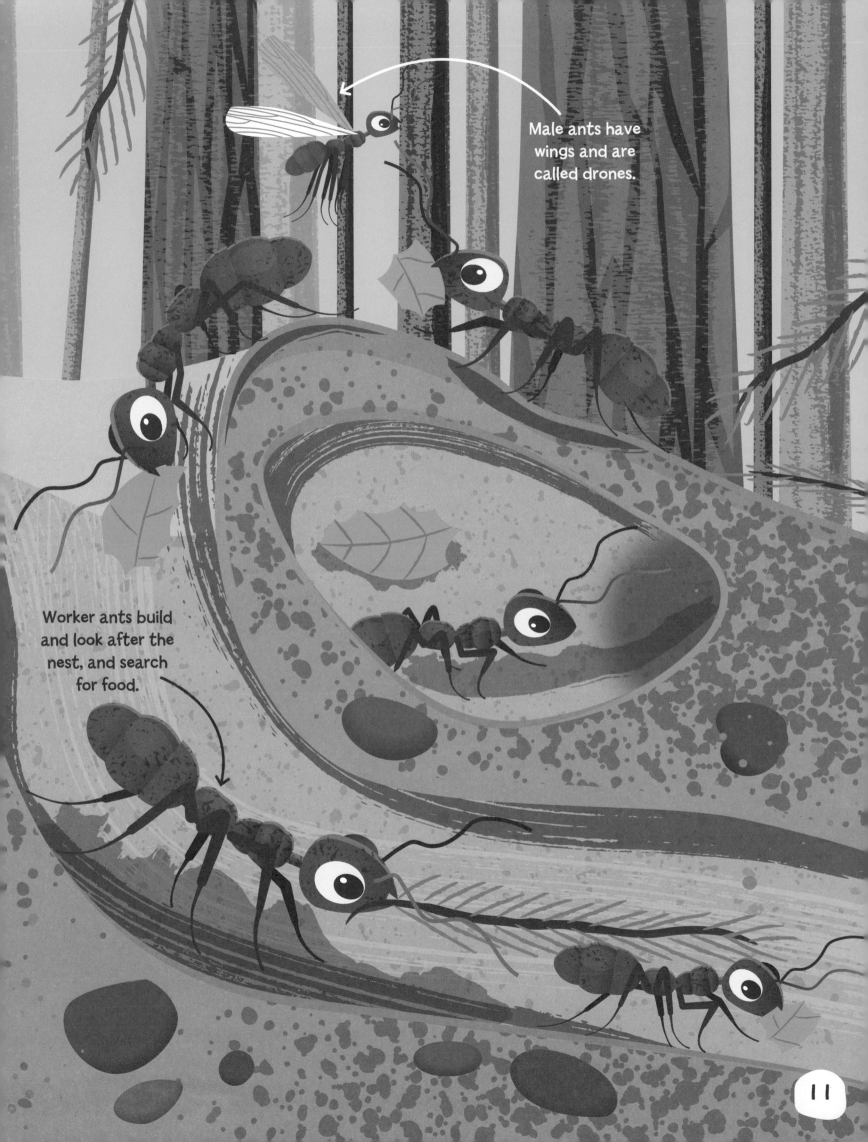

Male ants have wings and are called drones.

Worker ants build and look after the nest, and search for food.

HONEYBEE

Being a honeybee is a
BUSY, BUZZY BUSINESS.

Bees fly from flower to flower collecting sweet **nectar** to make into honey. They spread pollen as they go, helping plants to make new seeds.

See-through wings

Pollen sticks to the hair on their legs and body.

12

Take care – some bees have a stinger!

DID YOU KNOW?

I eat... nectar and pollen from flowers.

I have... 6 legs and 5 eyes!

I can be found... in forests, gardens, or meadows, where flowers grow.

I grow up to... 1 inch (25mm).

The antennae are used to touch, smell, and taste.

EARTHWORM

THESE WIGGLY, WRIGGLY WORMS LIVE UNDERGROUND.

They don't have any legs but are covered in tiny hairs, which help them **burrow** through the soil. Worms help to keep soil healthy, which is good for plants and other animals.

They don't have eyes, but can tell if it's light or dark.

DID YOU KNOW?

I eat... dead and rotting plants, and **microbes**.

I have... 0 legs!

I can be found... in damp soil.

I grow up to... 16 inches (40cm).

Poop comes out of this end.

14

Worms may not look very tasty, but birds love them!

Long tube-shaped body, made of lots of **segments**

Mouth

15

SNAIL

Snails are SOFT, SLIMY creatures with a hard shell on their back.

Snails are born with their shells and can curl up inside them to hide from danger. They normally live for 3 to 7 years.

Feelers help them find food.

Their shells are spiral shaped.

DID YOU KNOW?

I eat... plants and **fungi**. Sometimes I even eat worms, slugs, and other snails!

I have... 0 legs!

I can be found... in dark, damp places. Some of us even live in water.

I grow up to... 15 inches (38cm).

Inside its mouth are thousands of teeth.

Snails can be different sizes.

SLUG

Slugs are greedy guzzlers that will eat just about ANYTHING!

Most gardeners think they are real **pests** because they can cause a lot of damage to their plants. Slugs have soft, slimy bodies with no bones. They are like snails without a shell.

Feelers for seeing and smelling

Feelers for feeling and tasting

They leave slippery slime trails!

DID YOU KNOW?

I eat... plants and fungi. Sometimes I even eat worms, snails, and other slugs!

I have... O legs!

I can be found... in dark, damp, cool places.

I grow up to... 8 inches (20cm).

A slug's belly is called a foot.

SPIDER

Spiders are eight-legged CREEPY-CRAWLIES.

They are known for making webs, which you might have even seen in corners of your home! Different types of spiders are found all over the world, from dry deserts to your bathtub!

Spiders are clever creepy crawlies!

DID YOU KNOW?

I eat... mostly other bugs. Some very large tropical spiders can eat other small animals.

I have... 8 legs and 8 eyes!

I can be found... almost anywhere!

I grow up to... 11 inches (28cm).

They have a special body part, called a spinneret, that makes silk to spin their webs.

Spider silk is very strong!

FLY

There are THOUSANDS of different types of fly.

The buzzing sound flies make comes from their wings beating really fast. Most flies can flap their wings about 200 times a second!

DID YOU KNOW?

I eat... pollen and nectar from flowers, rotting plants and animals, and even poop.

I have... 6 legs!

I can be found... almost anywhere!

I grow up to... 3 inches (8cm).

Large eyes

Flies can taste with their feet!

Baby flies are called maggots. They look a bit like tiny worms.

Flies lay eggs on rotting plants and food.

When the eggs hatch, the baby flies have ready-made food to eat!

STICK INSECT

These bugs are HARD TO SPOT!

These insects really do look just like twigs. It helps them survive because other insects can't eat them if they don't know they're there!

They have very long, thin legs.

They let out a stinky smell and hissing sound when they get scared.

DID YOU KNOW?

I eat... plants, especially leaves and branches.

I have... 6 legs!

I can be found... in forests.

I grow up to... 25 inches (64cm).

Is it a stick or is it a bug?

If something grabs their leg, they'll let it drop off so they can escape. Don't worry, it will grow back!

DRAGONFLY

Dragonflies are skillful HUNTERS!

Dragonflies were one of the first winged insects to appear on our planet, around 300 million years ago. That's before dinosaurs existed!

They can fly backwards!

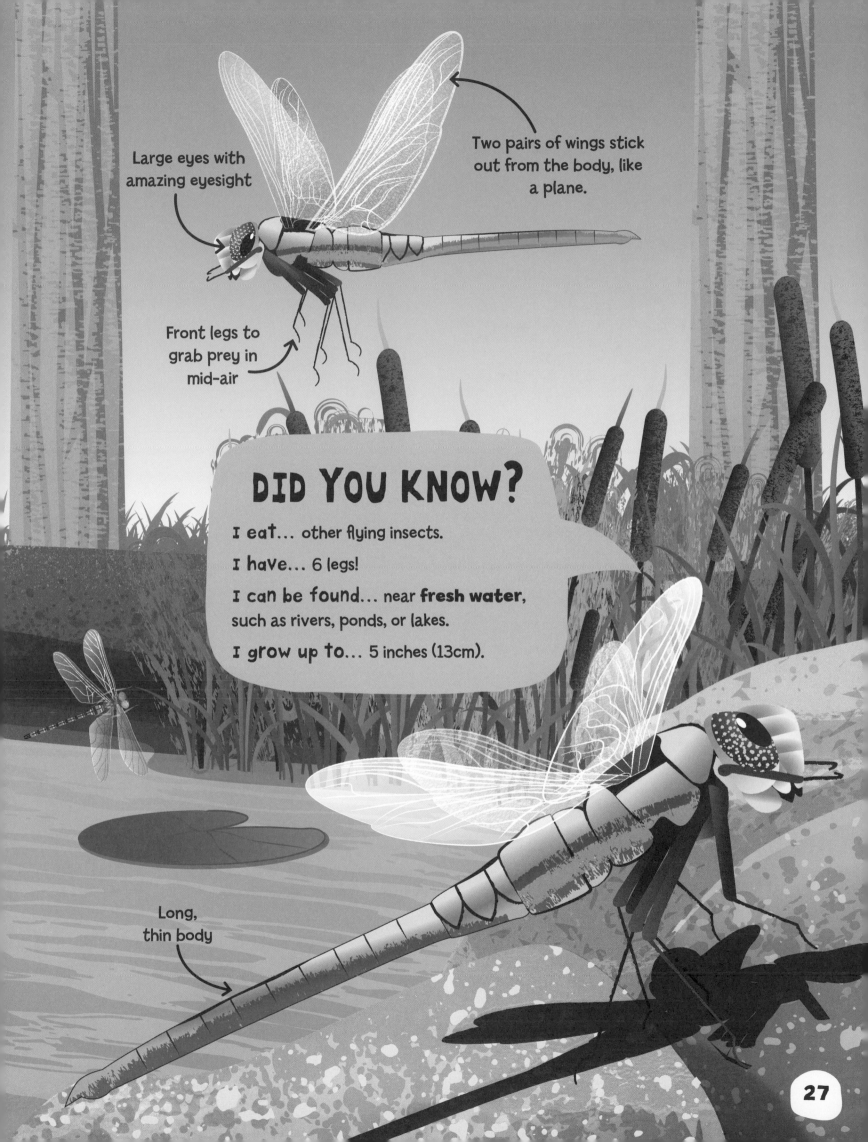

Large eyes with amazing eyesight

Two pairs of wings stick out from the body, like a plane.

Front legs to grab prey in mid-air

DID YOU KNOW?

I eat... other flying insects.

I have... 6 legs!

I can be found... near **fresh water**, such as rivers, ponds, or lakes.

I grow up to... 5 inches (13cm).

Long, thin body

MILLIPEDE
These LONG CREEPY-CRAWLIES have lots of legs.

Millipedes lay their eggs in the soil during spring and summer.
It takes just a few weeks for them to hatch into mini millipedes!

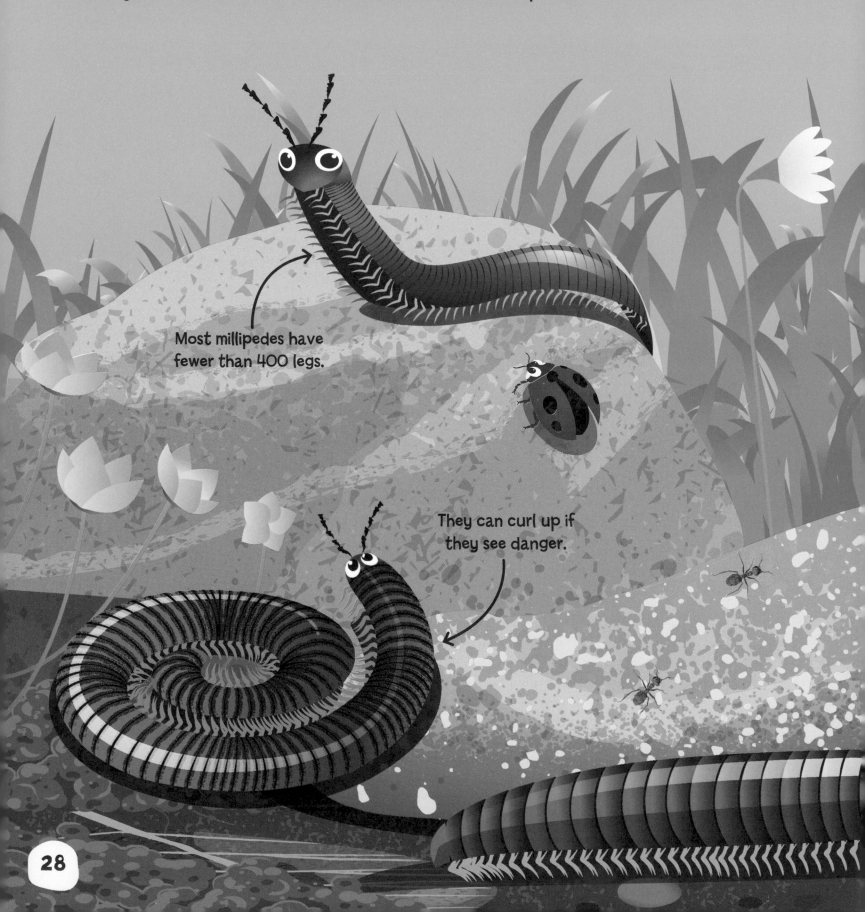

Most millipedes have fewer than 400 legs.

They can curl up if they see danger.

DID YOU KNOW?

I eat... dead and rotting plants, and wood.

I have... between 30 and 1,306 legs!

I can be found... mostly in forests.

I grow up to... 13 inches (34cm).

They have a hard outer shell.

BEETLES

These bright bugs help to keep soil HEALTHY!

They can look very different and come in lots of shapes and sizes. They have hard wing cases to protect their fragile wings.

Bright markings warn **predators** to stay away!

Stag beetles have mouthparts that look like antlers. They use them to fight other beetles.

Some beetles are bright and shiny, like beautiful gems.

DID YOU KNOW?

I eat... almost anything! Some of us eat plants, other insects, dead animals, or even poop!

I have... 6 legs!

I can be found... almost everywhere around the world.

I grow up to... 8 inches (19cm).

GRASSHOPPER

Grasshoppers use their strong back legs to JUMP!

Some of them can leap up to 20 times the length of their body. A human who could do that would be able to jump the length of a soccer field in a single jump! Grasshoppers are often found hiding in long grass.

Grasshoppers make a chirping noise by rubbing their wings against their back legs.

They hear sound through their belly!

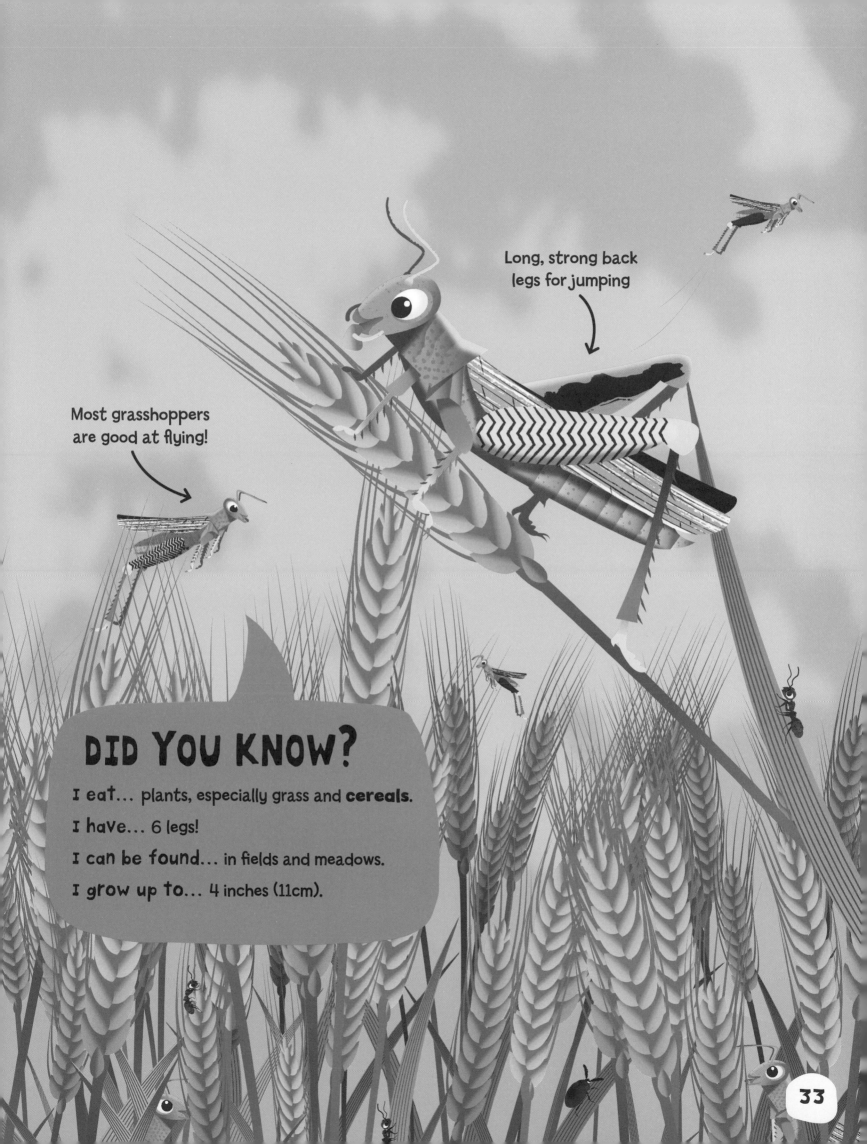

Long, strong back legs for jumping

Most grasshoppers are good at flying!

DID YOU KNOW?

I eat... plants, especially grass and **cereals**.

I have... 6 legs!

I can be found... in fields and meadows.

I grow up to... 4 inches (11cm).

CATERPILLAR

These GREEDY GRUBS spend almost all their time eating!

They may not look like it, but they are actually baby butterflies or moths. Once they are fully grown, they start to change into the completely different shape of a butterfly or moth ...wow! Turn the page to see what they turn into!

Bodies can be smooth or hairy.

Caterpillars have 6 legs, but they also have extra stumpy **prolegs** to help them move and grip onto things.

DID YOU KNOW?

I eat... plants, especially leaves, flowers, and fruit.

I have... 6 legs!

I can be found... almost anywhere!

I grow up to... 5 inches (13cm).

Caterpillars make a **chrysalis** like this to live in while they change shape!

BUTTERFLY

What bright and beautiful WINGS!

Can you believe this butterfly was once a caterpillar? Their wings can be lots of different patterns and shapes. Butterflies love to fly around in the sunshine, which helps to keep them warm.

Butterflies have four wings.

I'm going to be a butterfly soon!

DID YOU KNOW?

I eat... sweet liquids, including nectar, fruit juice, and tree sap.

I have... 6 legs!

I can be found... almost anywhere!

I grow up to... 11 inches (28cm).

Butterflies use their feet to taste!

Long, curled mouthpart for reaching nectar

Thin antennae help them smell and balance.

FIREFLY
These glowing bugs
LIGHT UP THE NIGHT!

These beautiful glow-in-the-dark bugs are not flies at all - they're beetles! They make their own light using special organs inside their bellies in order to send messages to each other.

Most fireflies are **nocturnal.**

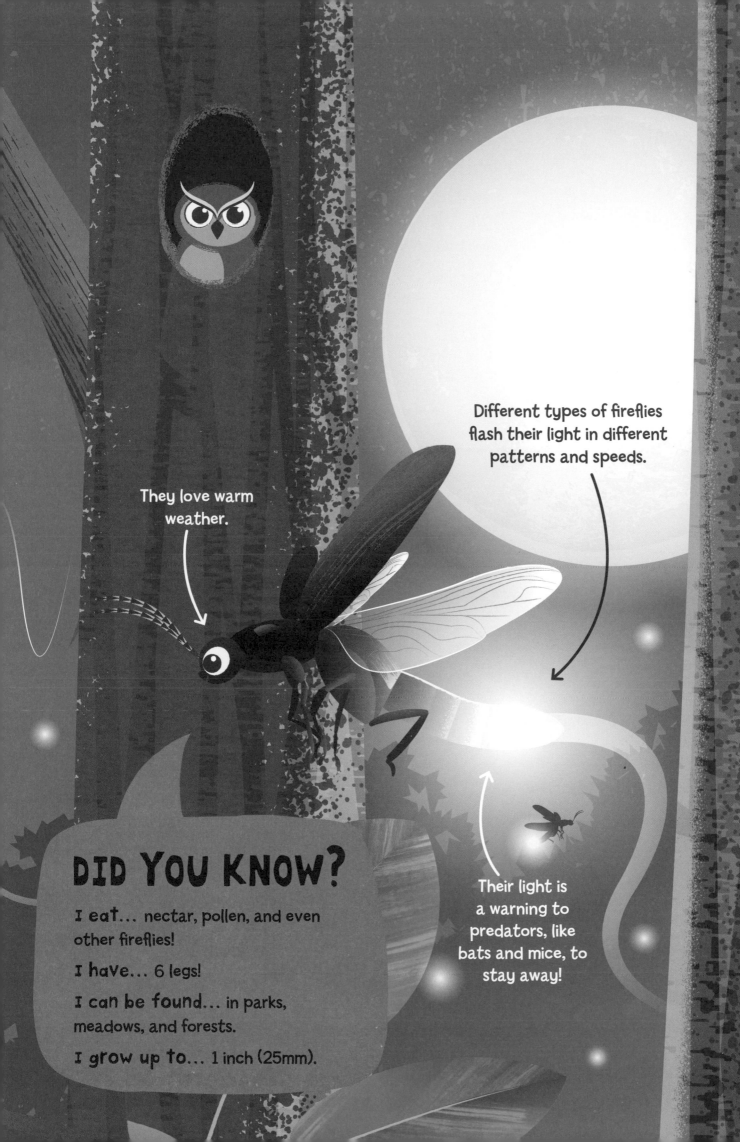

Different types of fireflies flash their light in different patterns and speeds.

They love warm weather.

DID YOU KNOW?

I eat... nectar, pollen, and even other fireflies!

I have... 6 legs!

I can be found... in parks, meadows, and forests.

I grow up to... 1 inch (25mm).

Their light is a warning to predators, like bats and mice, to stay away!

WHAT'S THAT BUG?

With millions of different types of bug out there, it can be difficult to tell them apart! Here's a chart to help you identify some of the different bugs mentioned in this book.

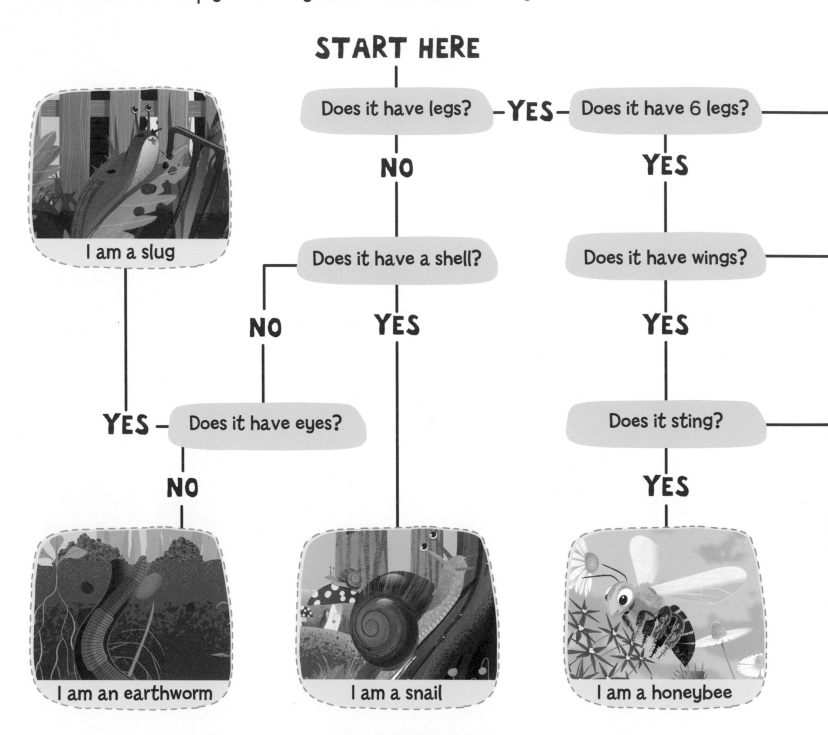

START HERE

Does it have legs? —YES— Does it have 6 legs?

NO

YES

Does it have a shell?

Does it have wings?

NO

YES

YES

I am a slug

Does it have eyes?

Does it sting?

YES

YES

NO

I am an earthworm

I am a snail

I am a honeybee

BUG HUNT

Go on a bug hunt around an outside space near you and see what bugs you can find. Make your own chart or take this one with you so you can identify them as you go along. Make sure to leave the bugs in their hiding places after you've finished identifying them!

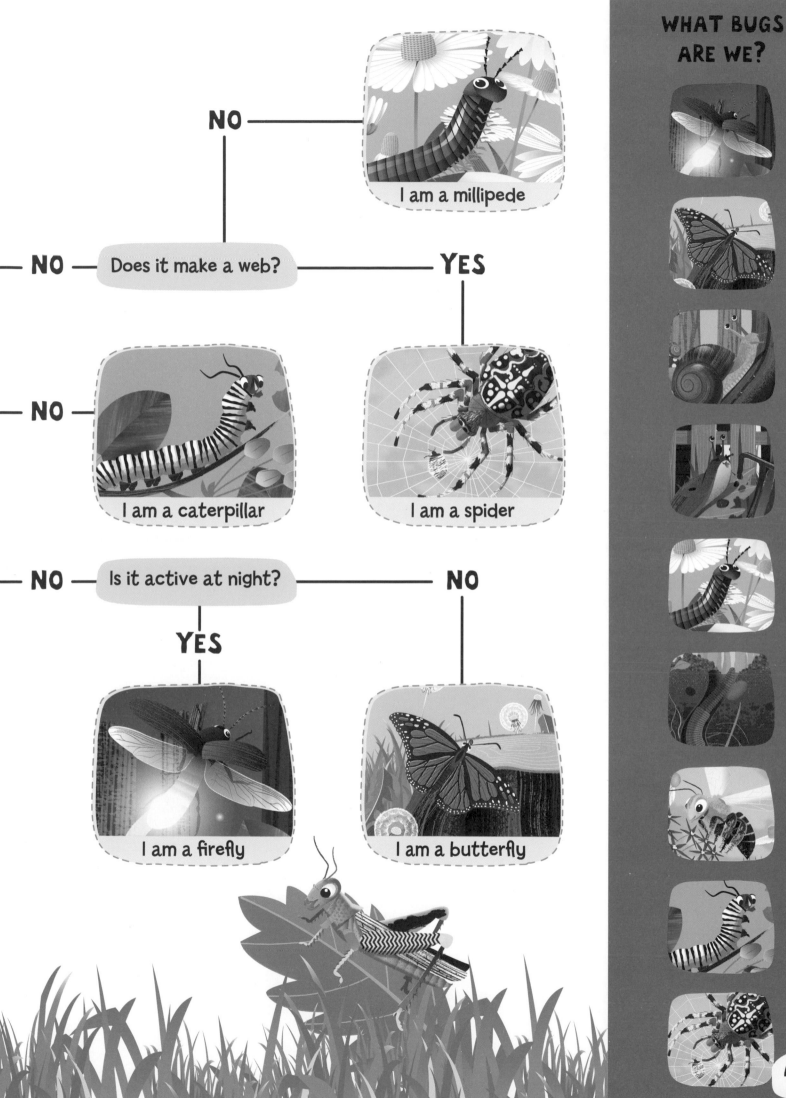

NO ——————————————— I am a millipede

NO ——— Does it make a web? ——————— YES

NO ——— I am a caterpillar

I am a spider

NO ——— Is it active at night? ——————— NO

YES

I am a firefly

I am a butterfly

41

WHY BUGS MATTER

Some people think bugs are scary or disgusting, but they all have an important part to play in the world we live in. Why are they important?

LOVE BUGS!

Without little bugs, our planet would be in big trouble! So, it's important to be kind and gentle to any bugs that you might meet.

SOIL SAVERS!

Bugs that live underground help to keep soil healthy by moving it around and eating up dead things in it. Even their poop helps plants grow!

PERFECT POLLINATORS!

Bees, butterflies, and many other insects are **pollinators**. They help spread pollen between flowers, which allows plants to make seeds and fruit.

BUGS FOR DINNER?

Many animals, like birds and bats, eat bugs. Without them, a lot of creatures would go hungry!

INDEX

First published in 2024 by Hungry Tomato Ltd.
F15, Old Bakery Studios, Blewetts Wharf,
Malpas Road, Truro, Cornwall, TR1 1QH, UK.

Illustrated by Dusan Lakicevic with help from Mark Ruffle

Thanks to our creative team:
Editor: Holly Thornton
Senior Designer: Amy Harvey

Copyright © 2024 Hungry Tomato Ltd

Beetle Books in an imprint of Hungry Tomato.

A CIP catalog record for this book is available from
the British Library.

ISBN:
9781915461162

Printed and bound in China

Discover more at
www.hungrytomato.com
www.mybeetlebooks.com

GLOSSARY

Burrow (verb) – to make a hole or tunnel, usually to live in.

Cereals – plants that produce edible grains, such as wheat, rice, and oats.

Chrysalis – a hard case that protects a caterpillar while it changes into a moth or butterfly.

Fungi – a group of living things, including mushrooms, truffles, and yeasts, that are neither plants nor animals.

Fresh water – natural water that doesn't contain salt. It is found in rivers, ponds, and lakes, but not in oceans.

Microbes – very small living things that can only be seen using a microscope.

Nectar – a sweet liquid that flowers make. Bees, butterflies, and some other insects eat it.

Nocturnal – creatures that sleep in the day and come out at night.

Pests – annoying or troublesome things. For example, bugs that eat people's plants and food are considererd pests.

Pollen – a dusty powder made by some flowers. Plants need pollen from flowers to make seeds.

Pollinators – insects and other animals that spread pollen between plants.

Predators – animals that hunt and kill other animals for food.

Proleg – small, fleshy body parts that look and act like legs but aren't actually legs.

Sap – a watery substance that comes out of a plant or tree.

Segments – pieces of something that can be separated.